The Maze
of Motherhood

The Maze of Motherhood

Real Stories of Real Moms:

Triumphs and Trials

Vol. 1

Jameliah Blount

HOLISTICALY EMPOWERED YOUTH

Published by: Holistically Empowered Youth, Inc.

www.heyyouthinc.com

Book Design: Jameliah Blount

Printed in the United States of America

« Dedication »

This book is dedicated to all mothers who take each and every moment with their children; good, bad, and the sometimes unexpected as a blessing. Believing that you become stronger and more empowered with each passing day. Continue to follow your dreams and help your children realize and develop dreams of their own.

To each of the moms that trusted me to share their stories. I appreciated you believing in me and being apart of my dream. Your honesty inspired me to push forward and to share more myself.

Lastly, I also dedicate this book to my "Thing 1 and Thing 2." Watching both of you grow and stretch yourselves to try new things outside of your comfort zones, fills my heart with such joy and daily motivation, to continue to push forward and be greater.

« INTRODUCTION »

Over the years, I have found that there are so many people who speak to the beauty and joy that bringing a new life into the world brings. They talk about the fulfillment and new found purpose that the little bundle of joy has added to their lives. All of this is true and I also have felt every moment of every one of those experiences twice.

There is also another piece to those beautiful and joyous feelings which includes the trying and sometimes difficult moments that we all face in the navigation of the maze of life.

As mothers, we are able to be participants in a miracle each time we experience giving birth. Each of our children are gifts from God. A gift that comes with great joy but also great sacrifices and sometimes difficulty. Each mother's path through the maze is different, but everyone can learn from the path that another mother has taken. I believe that it is our job to share our stories, moments, and experiences with others. Through the words written in this book and the conversations had after reading them. I hope that we each can help another mother learn to enjoy the process. Having the opportunity to have other moms contribute to this book was a real blessing and I am grateful. Their moments and experiences are what fueled the idea and the desire to continue to push through the setbacks.

When thinking of a title for this book, I began to think about the ups, downs, and the turns that we must take in our decision-making process each and every day to achieve our shared goal of raising our children to be holistically empowered and strong young adults. The happy moments plus the unpleasant experiences are what make us the best mom's that we can be.

« TABLE OF CONTENTS »

.

« Chapter 1: Mommy Journey »

"Today is a brand new day. My past does not define me. My future is mine to create. Anything I dream can come true."

A large part of becoming a mom for me was the journey that I took even before I made it to the hospital or experienced holding my son for the first time.

My beginnings…

My mommy journey began for me at the age of 20. I was dating my childhood crush. He and I had been friends for over 7 years before we ever dated. So when we finally did I just knew that through all the ups and downs in my previous relationships that this finally felt right. Our years of friendship had led us to this moment in time to explore what it would mean to be more than friends. When it came to relationships I was happier then I had been in a long time.

After dating for a few months, I began to feel very sick, cramping, exhausted, aching, and unable to hold anything down. My immediate thought was terror. "Was I pregnant?" No, I couldn't possibly be pregnant." I was on birth control. To ease my feelings, I purchased a home pregnancy test and the results were negative. I felt some relief, but I still wasn't feeling well. Unconvinced by the test. I scheduled an appointment to be checked by my gynecologist.

Over the next few days, I pushed through school and work while continuing to feel horrible. When the day finally came for my appointment, my doctor agreed that we should rule out pregnancy before looking into any other causes. He recommended that I have a physical exam and be given a urine and a blood test. After the exam and the urine test the doctor explained to me that I wasn't pregnant and that my cramping could just be normal hormonal changes. He prescribed some medications for me to take that would help to ease the symptoms. He still wanted me to take the blood test to make sure that there was no chance that I might still be pregnant. A few days went by and my blood test results once again showed that I wasn't pregnant.

Over the next few months, I continued to feel horrible with no ease or comfort even while taking the prescribed medications. In an effort to find out what was wrong with me, I scheduled an appointment with my general practitioner. Once at my appointment, I explained my symptoms and the fact that I had already received medication from my gynecologists. She took her time to listen to me and decided it was best for her to give me a physical as well. Within 2 minutes of my physical exam, the doctor stated she believed that there was a mass around my uterus and wanted me to have an ultrasound immediately.

She called over to the gynecologist who worked with her to see if they could fit me into their schedule. As soon as the doctor put the ultrasound scope on my belly, she saw a baby. Immediately filled with so many emotions. Happy that I finally had an answer as to why I felt so horrible, but terrified because I had no idea how I was going to tell my boyfriend nor what his reaction would be. After everything the other

2

doctors had told me; I was pregnant. This wasn't what we had planned and he was already not in the best place with his parents impending divorce.

After the ultrasound, the doctor gave me some important directives. Since I didn't know I was pregnant, I was prescribed several medications that shouldn't have been given to a pregnant woman. I was now considered a high-risk pregnancy needing to keep stress low, and would require increased monitoring throughout my pregnancy. I was also told that my child might be stunted, delayed, or have long term brain defects but we wouldn't know until his birth. After leaving the doctors, the first thing I did was call my mother and replay to her my appointment and now the increased risks. She told me that I was faithful and strong and that I could handle anything that God had given me. That night I told my boyfriend what happened and he completely shut down. The next day while we were talking via text he told me that he wasn't ready to be a father and that I should terminate the pregnancy. At that moment in all my pain, I made my first sacrifice as a mother and decided that my child's life and health was more important than any relationship. I knew the risks of stress to my unborn child, so I walked away from my boyfriend. I would not see him again until my son was a month old.

~ ~

"I didn't actually feel like a mom until I brought my baby girl home and it was our first night together. She was my first child and initially I just felt like I was "babysitting" her. She was, of course restless, hungry and dependent on this girl whom she's heard the voice of, but didn't really know. I bathed her, fed her and brushed her hair until she drifted off to sleep.

During the night, my sister came in and took a pic, unbeknownst to either my baby girl or me. In the morning, my sister returned to my room laughing. I'm asking what the joke is because needless to say; I'm exhausted.

She waves a picture at me, a Polaroid as this was the dark ages before camera phones, and tells me to "look at this."

I looked at the picture and saw myself fast asleep with one arm over both my eyes and laying on my other arm. My baby was beside me with, you may have guessed it, one arm over both her eyes and we were facing each other!! She was laying on her other arm as well with her tiny little hand wrapped around my finger!

At that moment I knew she was mine! I was her Mom, and no way did the hospital make a mistake."

~ ~

"My pregnancy was relatively normal. However, the delivery was another story. I was in labor for an entire weekend!!

My mom took me to the hospital twice, just to be sent home because they claimed I was in false labor. There was nothing fake about that pain!! I didn't eat nor drink anything for two days straight!! The pain was so unbearable because prior to that and ever since I never actually experienced any sort of excruciating pain. I've never broken any bones, had any stitches, no severe cuts, nothing. So to me, this was major!!

Finally, on Sunday, my mom took me back to the hospital and told my doctor that I am in no uncertain terms leaving with this baby inside me!! Go Mom!! Apparently, I was still in "false" labor, but my doctor felt sorry for me and was a little afraid of my mom, so he purposely broke my water which immediately brought on the delivery. My daughter came out, after two pushes, so fast that the doctor literally caught her in his forearms!! Swear to GOD!! It was so fast that I required 40 stitches to close me up!

I say that was a struggle! A beautiful struggle but a struggle, nonetheless."

~ ~

"My mommy journey began the moment my hubby, and I decided to start our family. We had no way of knowing how quickly we would get pregnant, but it happened much sooner than either of us expected. When the pregnancy was confirmed, we were both a little shocked, euphoric and eager to share the news with our family."

~ ~

"The beginning of my mommy journey started with the decision to stop taking birth control. My husband and I thought that we were ready to start a family. However, once the pregnancy happened that was so far from the truth at least for him. I believe that was when I lost my husband. His focus baby quickly shifted off of me and the baby and he began to solely focus on himself. As the baby grew in my stomach so did my love for her. I knew at that time I would do anything for her. She finally arrived one month pass my due date after 24 hours of labor, and a very angry phone call from my mother, and a C-section. My beautiful daughter was in my arms."

~ ~

"Both of my pregnancies were without incident. I think I struggled the most after births. Following my first child, I developed problems with my gallbladder which eventually led to having it removed. Then my second husband and I went through a miscarriage which left me a little depressed. That quickly changed with the pregnancy of my second daughter. However, following her, I had complications with my uterus which then had to be removed. I can admit it took me a minute to bounce back. But most importantly I wanted to make sure the baby and I were okay."

~ ~

"My first pregnancy was worry free. It was an enjoyable experience. Like a lot of new moms and dads, we took classes to help prepare us for our new addition. One of the most valuable classes we took was the Hypnobirthing Class. The class taught breathing and relaxation techniques to use during delivery. I wanted to avoid an epidural, so the methods were especially helpful once labor set in. Having my hubby there beside me, coaching me through my labor helped keep me calm."

~ ~

Pregnancy moves so quickly that when we talk to our friends and family after the experience is over we forget that there was a journey of questions and decisions that we made to get us to that miraculous day. Other mom's journey starts once they have heard their babies' first cries or held them for the first time. There are also those moms that it takes a little longer to really feel like a mother. For them, it might be the first sleepless night or the first time they mastered breastfeeding. No matter how it begins, it is a memory that you will remember for the rest of your life.

Now write your own beginnings story…

_____

_____

_____

_____

_____

_____

_____

_____

_____

_____

_____

_____

_____

_____

_____

_____

_____

_____

_____

_____

_____

_____

_____

_____

_____

_____

_____

_____

_____

_____

_____

_____

_____

_____

_____

_____

_____

_____

_____

_____

« Chapter 2: Mommy Guilt »

"Taking care of yourself is part of taking care of your kids."

As a mother on a daily basis, we are required to make choices. We all start our journey with an idea of the type of mother that we want to be. Some want to be at home for every moment of their child's upbringing. Other moms have the desire to not only be great mothers but also continue to contribute to the business community as well. Moms sometimes have moments where they feel guilty for what they have to give up for not being home or for taking time out for themselves.

My Mommy Guilt...

Though I was now a single parent, I learned quickly about sacrifice and that there were going to be many choices that I would make for him. Initially, I was living on my own in a one bedroom apartment, working full time in a leasing office, and in college full time working on my bachelor's degree. Prior to all of this, my relationship with my parents was ok but not as strong as it had been in the past. As I grew older, I felt like I knew everything and could handle anything without any help. Having my son changed everything I believed that I had figured out about family and relationships.

Like every family, we have had our struggles especially when I felt it was time to show my independence, but no matter the growing pains I put them all through, they have always proved to be an amazing support system for me and my son. Deep down I felt like it was still my responsibility to provide for us. How could I ask my parents to help me take care of my child when I made the decisions which put my life on a different path? They didn't condone my decisions but they loved me and loved their grandson. Through it all, I was his mother, and I would make it work. So I would work 45+ hours a week, still maintain a full time schedule in school, and function as a mother of a new born.

During this time I was always exhausted. I know as moms we all feel at one time or another "mommy guilt." I was working, going to class, coming home to take care of home and spend time with my son, and then staying up late to get homework completed. I remember a pivotal moment during this time when my mother sat me down and told me that I was doing a good job. She reminded me not to feel bad because the sacrifices of time spent with my son as he was still little and really didn't understand. He knew and felt that I loved him. I was working to create the best life for him and that it would pull me away from him now but it would be worth it later. She also told me to fill every moment that I have with him with quality. So I set to fill our time together with amazing moments to remember.

~ ~

"With my second child, I was fortunate enough to be a stay-at-home mom for his first two years. But with my first, I had to put her in daycare at 2 months old. It was the hardest decision I had to make thus far. She went to a home daycare run by an older woman who was a friend of my mother's. That gave me some peace of mind because she wasn't a total stranger.

The first day I dropped her off, I arrived and of course stated all the things she needed to know to take care of my heart for the day before I handed her over. As soon as I let go, the screams were deafening! She turned the darkest shade of red I'd ever seen. I had to go to work, that wasn't even an option, so mommy guilt took over my entire spirit. Even though when I picked her up she was sleeping peacefully, the knowledge that I would have to go through that again the very next day was super saddening. But like a trooper, I dealt with the guilt and her crying when I left for the first two weeks. I didn't really feel the need to compensate in any way; I knew it was just separation anxiety. Now I'm going through it with my puppy."

~ ~

"My first husband left right after my daughter was born. But God saw fit to put someone in our lives. God sent someone to love me and my daughter. A good person, who only wanted the best for us. Still hurting and a little angry. I felt it was me and her against the world.

I felt like I had to be her mother and father. So to compensate I gave her whatever she wanted or what I felt like she needed. I became defensive and overprotective. Feeling like I let her down made it difficult to see the blessing that right in front of me. Vowing to never let anyone hurt us. It took a while to let someone else become her father and my husband; 4 years to be exact. God knew what was best even when I didn't."

~ ~

"My divorce hit me like a ton of bricks. For a long time, I felt like I couldn't breathe. Playing over and over in my head what I could have done differently. I was afraid of the ramifications that this would have on me but, more importantly, my children. The pain that I felt kept me extremely drained and tired. I continued to maintain as well as I could. I would take the kids to school and continued working. I would find myself crying in my office and crying at night. When I would get home with the boys, I was so disappointed in myself that I would just go to bed. I felt like I slept for days at a time. Like I said earlier just maintaining. As I began to come out of the fog, I realized how much time I had wasted. He was no longer there, but I needed to be present. They needed to feel my presence. They needed me to do more than just maintain. They needed me to live."

~ ~

We have to remember that our children are important to us; to many the most important. We give and give of ourselves to them and forget that we must be refilled and refreshed. The feeling of guilt comes from not recognizing that you need to take time out for yourself. This time allows you to rebuild your reserves so you can give more healthy attention and to be present with your children.

Now write about your own experience with mommy guilt…

_____

_____

_____

_____

_____

_____

_____

_____

_____

_____

_____

_____

_____

_____

_____

_____

_____

_____

_____

_____

_____

_____

_____

_____

_____

_____

_____

_____

_____

_____

_____

_____

_____

_____

_____

_____

_____

_____

« Chapter 3: Do you believe you are a Good Mother? »

"Not loving every moment of motherhood doesn't mean I
don't love being a mom."

Doubt is a sticky feeling that tries to creep in when
you least expect it. While preparing to become a mother,
most moms have a moment when they wonder if they would
be a good mother. They reflect on their mothers and wonder
if they could be as good as her or better than she was. Once
becoming a mom, every so often you look at them after
making a big decision and doubt if you are making the right
choices to give them the best chance for the best possible life.
During this time, I am always reminded of the child that is
sitting on the side of the pond throwing rocks into the water.
If you take a moment and watch, with each rock hitting the
water you see ripples that spread out after the original impact.
As a mother, I want to cause the least amount of damaging
future ripples in my children's lives.

My Mommy Doubt…

Doubt is something that I struggled with a lot
surrounding having my first son. Particularly the doubt of
"am I a good mother?" Was I making the right choices? Was
I raising my son to know that he could do anything that he
put his mind to? It wasn't like I grew up in a family that I
didn't have an amazing mother. A mother who always put my

sister and me first. Always making her own sacrifices to make sure that we were always taken care of. Yet looking back at this time in my life I can see that I made a lot of decisions based on this doubt. These decision would later change the course of our lives and move us into an entirely different directions.

For example, when my son was little I over compensated for my doubt. He had everything that he could ever need as a child and probably more from clothes to toys and everything else. At a time where I could have been saving money, I decided to move us into a larger apartment. Not because we didn't have enough space as it was just the two of us but because I believed that he had to have his own room. By the way, he wasn't even sleeping in the room at the time we moved. There was a point that I began to doubt the amount of time that I was spending with my son. This feeling sent me on a mission to start looking for a new job which would give me more awake hours and better benefits for us.

On the surface, there wasn't anything wrong with this idea. I allowed the doubt to move me ahead of God's time. I became so unhappy at my current position that when a new opportunity came along, I jumped at it. I believed myself to be naturally a person who compares all decisions that I make. So when I say I jumped, I really mean I created my list of pros and cons and then decided because I was unhappy this must be the best next step for us. Needless to say, I spent 9 years at the new job, and 5 of them were plagued with dismay. I worked more hours than I could count and there were many days that I only saw my family in the morning. Even though this choice was ahead of my time, it did provide for my household for those 9 years. I learned more about myself through those times then I think I would have learned if I had never experienced it. This doubt didn't just go away but as I continued to make each decision, I began to look at how this would affect us all. Each time my son was successful, it gave me more and more confidence in my parenting and the choices that I was making.

~ ~

"I had excellent role models to emulate what a good mother is. Not only my own mom, but I have three sisters, all older, who not only taught me how to take care of children but also had hands in raising me. So I received experience and discipline from both sides of the coin.

My oldest sister had her first and only child at a very young age. Nevertheless, she kept moving forward and up in her life. She moved out of my parent's house, went to night school and earned her bachelor's in Engineering. She did all this as a single parent. From that, I learned tenacity.

My second to the oldest sister was a little rough around the edges and didn't quite take the responsibility of raising her son as seriously. The majority of his adolescence was shaped by the rest of our family. From that, I learned culpability.

My third sister developed a disease in her early teens that limited her ability to work on a regular basis. She married and had three sons that were able to be at home with every day. She was so close to them, and they were close to each other, and it was evident to all who met them. She raised three responsible, humble and independent young me and from that I learned selflessness."

~ ~

"I often doubt myself, and whether or not I am doing a good job as a mother. In those times I seek feedback from trusted family and friends. I also remind myself that

because I care about the job I'm doing as a mother, I'm already doing a good job. I'm always reassured when someone compliments me on how well behaved or manner able my sons are."

~ ~

"If I considered anything a doubt it would be could I really still follow my dreams and still be a good mother. I have always known that I was destined for great things. Now that I am a mom would that have to end? Would I have to not pursue my dreams? Did I waste my time? What I realized that my children became my motivation to keep going and to keep dreaming. They were the catalyst that continued to remain me that I could do anything. They would just be along for the ride. Whenever I accomplish something new they are there to tell me how proud they are of me."

~ ~

I believe that doubt has to exist in some form. Without doubt, you can become accustomed to where you are. Doubt pushes you to make a decision and take action. Once you take the action, it gives you the momentum to continue forward and grow bigger and better. You realize that you can handle more and be just that much of a better mom.

Now write about a time you might have felt doubtful…

_____

_____

_____

_____

_____

_____

_____

_____

_____

_____

_____

_____

_____

_____

_____

_____

_____

_____

_____

_____

_____

_____

_____

_____

_____

_____

_____

_____

_____

_____

_____

_____

_____

_____

_____

_____

_____

_____

_____

_____

_____

« Chapter 4: Single, Married, Divorced, Re-Married, & Bonus Moms »

"I am adequate and equipped at all time to do that which is required of me no matter my status or current situation."

The most basic component that makes up life is that of change. The above quote is so important to be reminded of. Life changes, and with each change, we experience new levels of being a woman and the title of mom never changes. Motherhood is a status that transcends any relationship status. When the relationship ends or new relationship blossoms, we carry our children through it with us.

My mommy status transitions…

I can say that I have been a single mom, a married/bonus mom, and now a divorced mom. For me, this isn't something that I am proud to say, but it is the reality of my life. Each status has required me to stretch myself and to be a different type of mom. As a single mom, it was all on me to make sure everything was taken care of and that all of his needs were met all the time. Being a single mom came with its own level of stress and anxiety. When I got married, the single mother that I had become had some company and someone else there to bounce ideas off and help with the day to day rearing. As excited as I was to be married and to share my life with someone that I loved. The transition was tough. I had spent 2 years creating a parenting environment for my son and now there was someone else there bringing their own ideas of how my child should be raised and how a household should run. I had to give up some of my control which isn't something that I was completely ready to do when we first were married. As time went on, we continued to communicate finding where we agreed and where we disagreed. We began to find a rhythm. At least that is what I thought. What I hadn't realized was that I had given up my power. I wanted so badly to be a good wife and mother that I lost myself in it all. I no longer knew what made me happy. Everything I did was for them, and I became empty and unfulfilled.

After 7 years of marriage, I became a divorced mom. This was devastating to my world. I didn't know how I would make it through the change and if the boys would be ok. You hear so many stories about children who's parents have gotten divorced and it ruined them for the future. You also have those situations where the parents stayed together, and it had the same effect on the children. In my personal experience even though I had to deal with my own issues, it helped me to focus on the children's development first, knowing that I needed to keep their lives as consistent as possible with all the changes. So we continued our regular schedule church on Sundays, bible study on Tuesdays, they stayed at their school and continued all of their extra-curricular activities. The initial changes were tough on me because I didn't have that other person to take them to practices or clubs or to attend games. But even as tired as I was it brought me so much joy to see them thriving. I knew that I was still a good mom. Especially when my oldest son came to me and said, "mommy, I am so glad that I get to see you happy and smiling."

~ ~

"I did not marry until I was 30 with two kids. I met and married a man who also had two children who came with him. Taking care of a household of 6 is far from easy and not always rewarding. Four mouths to feed, four homework papers to help write, four kids to get ready for school and four participants of football and cheerleading every year.

I'm glad someone came up with the title "bonus mom" to replace stepmom because it truly is "extra". Extra love, extra laughs, extra support, and extra responsibility. I naturally treated my bonus kids exactly like my biological children because, at the end of the day, they're just kids who need and love you. If their biological mom is not in their lives for whatever reason, they need a mom figure to handle mom things. I never made them feel like they were "less than my own."

When their father and I divorced, I realized that I was the only one in the relationship, directly and indirectly, who felt that way because my kids never see that side of our blended family again, and I never saw my bonus kids again. It wasn't due to any action or non-action on my part, they were literally told that part of their lives was over. It hurt, but it's all good, for 8 years I helped mold and shape them into the people they are today. I did that."

~ ~

"There was a period of time where I had to determine who I was again. For some time I was married and knew my role. When I became divorced, I continued to care for my daughter but lost myself. The divorce took a lot out of me. I was alone, young and depressed. I worked, partied or in a corner crying. This was my existence for a while. My family lived in another state. Being in the military made me strong and determined to survive. I decided to make living in a place I knew nothing about work.

I didn't have help, so I struggled with knowing how to care for her as a mother. I can say it was a lot through trial and error. Without having a support system, I did everything myself. I walked pass my job to the babysitter then back to work; at the end of the day, I walked to the babysitter, pick up my daughter, back pass work to get home every day. Money was tight and no help.

We spent a lot of time home alone. I worried a lot and was terrified who would miss us. Who would even know if something happened? Did I say I cried a lot? I also thought about suicide. My concern for her wellbeing and conversation with an unknown voice, who I have come to know was God; dried every tear, calmed my fears, and even though I was still scared, he picked me up and sent me to work (forward) every day. For me, it was she and I against the world, and we were going to be okay.

In answers to my prayers God sent James. We became good friends, my daughter was about 6 months old. He encouraged me, supported me; not financially but with the Love of God. He lived in Philadelphia on a Navy ship, but every opportunity he had. Mostly weekends he visited. He helped me learn my way around, he sent me home to see my mom, and we spent time with his family who welcomed us in. Still a little hesitant we eventually became a family. He gave her the father she deserved."

~ ~

"I've only been a married mom, so I know what that entails. However, as a military spouse, I often function as a single mother, when my hubby is deployed. I have the unique experience of knowing what it's like to have your spouse there to assist with childcare, and how challenging it can be by yourself."

~ ~

Change is the one constant when you are a mom. Nothing is ever staying the same. You never get enough sleep, and they are continuously growing. As my baby continues to grow the relationships around me continued to change as well. I had to begin to adjust where I spent my time, energy, and money. I had to choose between my selfish singles ways and focus all my energy towards my family.

How have you handled your status? ...

_____

_____

_____

_____

_____

_____

_____

_____

_____

_____

_____

_____

_____

_____

_____

_____

_____

_____

_____

_____

_____

_____

_____

_____

_____

_____

_____

_____

_____

_____

_____

_____

_____

_____

_____

_____

_____

_____

_____

_____

_____

_____

_____

« Chapter 5: What's in a name? »

"Don't name your Future by your Present circumstances."

- Steve Harvey

The name game is a fun and sometimes grueling process when you're pregnant. Do you pick a name from a list or do you name them after someone important to you? When do you tell people the name? These are all questions asked during the process of naming your children. But for everyone, this is one of the most important decisions you will make.

My mommy name "Game"…

I have two sons but the circumstances around choosing their names were entirely different experiences. My oldest son was born during a time in my life where I was single and learning my own strength. I knew that I wanted his name to have a biblical reference, but I didn't want something traditionally holy. As I began to look through the names, I saw the name Jordan for the Jordan River. In the bible, the Jordan River was the location for several miracles. Jordan is my miracle child. He was said to have disabilities, and long-term effects from pregnancy, but today he is a bright, and loving little boy with a love of science and engineering. Though somewhat traditional, his middle name came from naming him after a family member near and dear to my heart, my father, James.

Now my youngest son was born surrounding different circumstances. I was married, so I didn't have a complete say in what his name was going to be, but it was a lot more fun. When we first started looking at names my husband just knew that we were going to have a girl. That list was short and easy for us to agree on. When we went for our sonogram and found out that we were having another boy, the naming became just that much more challenging. We each had a son already that started with J, so it just made more sense for us to continue the J naming since we were going to have 3 sons. We were able to get the list to one set of letters, but it wasn't any easier from there. My husband wasn't so thrilled with the idea of getting another name from the bible. So we each went through the baby name book, put our favorites on sticky notes on a wall in our bedroom. Every so often we would agree on a name that we both didn't like and cross it off the list. By the time we got down to the last two names; he had one and I had one, so we folded the two names up and had my god sister pick to determine the name. She picked Jackson.

As I look at him now, the other name would have never worked. The name speaks to everything that Jackson, to me stands for; strength, stoic, and caring. His middle name was an easy pick. Since my husband's name was selected for the first name, he let me pick the middle. My first name began with J, and his first name was C, so it made sense to have the baby's middle name began with a C as well. So it was a no-brainer for me, "Christian" it is.

~ ~

"It is amazing how many people do not really know the meaning of their child's name. I heard a name that really stuck with me. So while in the hospital I gave the nurse the name but really didn't know how to spell it. So she did. It means "beautiful" and she is inside and out. My second daughter came along when Aladdin was out, and of course Jasmine was it. I worked with a person who was happy, bubbly and energetic all the time so I gave her his last name as her middle name. She is truly my flower that loves adventure and is full of life she brings joy (Happy and Bubbly)"

~ ~

"While pregnant with our oldest son, I asked my husband if he wanted a junior, prior to finding out the baby's gender. Initially, my husband said no, and we proceeded to consider other names. We'd decided on Emory Chace when my husband was convinced by his mother that he should name our baby after himself. I was upset because I felt that our understanding and agreement that the baby wouldn't be a junior had been voided. I was disappointed that after months of considering other names and agreeing on a different name, that my husband could so easily be influenced to change his mind. At times over the years, it has bothered me still, but when I look at our son and witness the bond he shares with his father, I'm happy they share the same name.

As for our middle son, when we confirmed I was pregnant with him, I felt for sure he would be a boy. My pregnancy symptoms were eerily similar to my first pregnancy with our eldest son. We made a list of names that we liked, shared them with family for their input and finally decided on a first name we both loved. We chose to honor my father by giving our son his name as well. It was the best decision, because as our little "Moses" has grown, he's exhibited traits just like his grandpa's."

~ ~

The name you pick will travel with your child for the rest of their lives. It will become a preceding statement as to who they are in the world. Their name will be the first thing that people know about them, the first thing seen on a resume. We all have one time or another where we look up our names to see what they mean. Looking to see if the meaning of the name really reflects who we are.

Now write about how you named your child? …

_____

_____

_____

_____

_____

_____

_____

_____

_____

_____

_____

_____

_____

_____

_____

_____

_____

_____

_____

_____

_____

_____

_____

_____

_____

_____

_____

_____

_____

_____

_____

_____

_____

_____

_____

_____

_____

_____

_____

_____

_____

_____

_____

_____

« Chapter 6: Mommy Success »

"A mother's dream is to see her children grow to be happy and successful."

Of the moms I spoke to, many of them told me that seeing their children succeed is not only their greatest joy but also their biggest success.

Mommy success moment…

For me as a mom, I feel successful when the children are successful. It is probably cliché and most moms feel that way, but I spend a lot of time with my children on what they consider their dreams or, as I call, them their current passions. I say what they feel are their dreams because something that I have learned is that they are 9 and 5. Every day they love something new and no longer like something that they previously enjoyed. So I have taken the time to learn the signs of when my children are moving onto something else. Sometimes they genuinely no longer have an interest, and other times they are moving on because they don't want to do the work. Knowing the difference has saved me in which changes to fight and which to let go.

So every sports games that they win or learn a new skill. At every karate belt testing ceremony where they get to see the fruit of all those classes. At a school program where we have worked for days learning to memorize lines. In the mornings when they are taking a school project in for grading. I know that they have worked hard to exceed the requirements I can smile. I can think to myself that they are becoming better young men with each success they accomplish, and I am becoming a better mom with each success I watch them achieve. In that same breath, when they don't quite make their goals it gives me a chance to remind them that there is always next time. We can always work a little harder for a yes.

These conversations are always a reminder to myself too. That sometimes I get it right the first time and sometimes I have to try over and over again and learn from each bad experience to become better. An example of this is that my son is an actor, early on he was too young to know really what was going on at an audition. He would just go to laugh or smile, and they loved or didn't love him. Sometimes we would get a callback and sometimes we wouldn't but it didn't matter to him. He would just go on and be a happy baby. As he has gotten older the auditions, become more work, and his perfectionist nature has begun to play a bigger role. So he wants to know why he was selected and when he's not selected he wants to know why he wasn't. Knowing what he did wrong helped him to know what not to do the next time. So now, he works so much harder on his monologue or his audition materials and he walks into the room confident. They are the most rewarding. These are lessons that a conversation couldn't teach him. It doesn't matter to me if he books the job or not but the confidence that he displays will transfer into everything he does for the rest of his life.

~ ~

"I get my best "mom's all that" success story from my kids. I had decided to separate finally and divorce my husband and was searching for a new place to live. As a result of that search, I found out that my husband was not handling the finances as he should and that our track record for paying rent on time was more than challenged.

I was being denied left and right and was very close to seeing myself as homeless. Not so much living outside because I had family that would help but not being approved for a place of my own. My kids would have to change schools and move away from friends. By this time they were in middle school and at the age of transition.

Being the woman/mom that I was taught to be, I battled through the denials and finally got approval for our own place. But the best part is I only had to move across the parking lot of the place I shared with my husband and his kids. The complex understood that I wasn't the one signing checks and that if given the opportunity, I would not repeat my husband's errors. So we moved across the parking lot to an apartment, my kids stayed in the same school with the same friends and our lives got totally better! All because their mom was not going to let them down as a result of a situation they had no control over."

~ ~

"My proud moments would me now. I watch my oldest go through some of the hardest times of her life. I watch her grow closer to God and follow his lead. I watch her continue to love and nurture her boys. I watch her continue to move forward. I'm watching her grow and become stronger as a woman and a mother.

My youngest is walking in her dreams. She is finishing school, and working. She is loving kind and respectful. She loved God and have a relationship with Him. I am most proud that they have each other and support one another."

~ ~

"My oldest son received an A/B Honor Roll certificate last school year. I was so proud of him, because just a few weeks before school began, we relocated, moved into a new home, and had very little downtime to get acquainted with our new environment. Despite the abruptness of it all, he still managed to excel at school and make new friends. I was proud of myself for being able to support him throughout the changes while organizing a new home and caring for two other small children. As they say, "teamwork makes the dream work!"

~ ~

Something that I practice frequently is to enjoy every moment of success. Whenever I have a moment to laugh, smile, and feel joy, I try to enjoy it. Like we have already discussed when raising children everything is always changing. The changes are sometimes for the good and the bad. So make sure to stop and take a moment to enjoy it, remember it, and even write it down.

What mom success stories do you want to remember? ...

_____

_____

_____

_____

_____

_____

_____

_____

_____

_____

_____

_____

_____

_____

_____

_____

_____

_____

_____

_____

The Maze of Motherhood

_____

_____

_____

_____

_____

_____

_____

_____

_____

_____

_____

_____

_____

_____

_____

_____

_____

_____

_____

_____

_____

_____

_____

« Chapter 7: Mom Learning Lessons »

"No regrets in life. Just lessons learned."

Through struggle and sacrifice, we find the strength that we never knew existed. We find the people that are there to support us and help guide us through the pain. We see the true nature of people we need to remove from our space. We are able to come out on the other side of the situation and not only learn a lesson that will change our lives but be able to tell our story to someone else so that they might not have to endure the struggle.

A few of my mommy lessons learned...

I learned the most about myself and about being a mom from the failures that I have encountered. Let me first say that that by failure I mean those things that didn't live up to my expectations of an outcome. Most of my situations are not dictionary definitions of a failure but is something that made me feel that way.

When my oldest was about 2, we went to the dentist for our first appointment. Thinking nothing of it other than it was a regular part of life for a toddler. You automatically schedule to go to the doctors, and then the dentist. While at this appointment they told me that my son has soft teeth. Something that I had never heard of and that he had cavities.

He would need caps on his front two teeth. I was devastated so much, so I burst into tears at the office. The idea that you were going to have to drill in his mouth to fix them and then cap them. At the time he was also modeling and what his smile looked like mattered. It took the dentist and my mother telling me that this was normal for some children to have soft teeth. I had done everything that I could by brushing his teeth twice a day, but some kids are just prone to cavities. It was an experience. When I had my second son, I was aware of the possibilities and took extra precautions as well as began our dentist visits at one instead of waiting.

~ ~

It was an ordinary night in the house. The boys were playing well together, and I was watching a movie. Unusually quiet in a typically loud home. When my baby boy walks up to me crying hysterically. I look at him and ask him why he is upset. In the midst of his tears says that he swallowed a penny. I think I had a moment of shock and asked him to repeat himself. And he says to me, "Mommy, I swallowed a penny." I immediately called my parents who have medical backgrounds and can typically tell me if I should freak out or not. They asked me how he felt and if he could breathe. I said yes he could and then I asked him how he felt. He told me his chest was hurting. I touched his chest, and I could feel the penny in his chest. I immediately got the children dressed and rushed to the emergency room. Once we got there, they said that this happens a lot and not to freak out. We went back for an x-ray and found out that the penny was stuck in his chest. He needed to try to eat and drink so that it could move the penny down. The emergency room staff was fantastic making sure to make him feel comfortable and even gave him copies of his x-rays as a souvenir. So needless to say, we had a very long conversation about what is considered food and what isn't and what goes in your nose and what shouldn't. My lesson in all this was that no matter how old they get you can't assume that the basic lessons still don't need to be addressed again.

~ ~

"The one and only time I felt like a complete failure as a mom was when my son was 3 years old. I, my daughter and son and my son' dad had been living together for 5 years. My son was three years old when I decided that the relationship was no longer healthy and that his dad needs to move out. At the time, my son was being cared for while we worked by his aunt on his father's side, free of charge.

Once his family got wind of our separation and because his moving out was not mutual, he convinced his aunt to no longer watch my son for me but only do it if I allowed my son to move out with him. Being between and rock and a hard place was an understatement. I was not earning enough to pay the household expenses, childcare for my daughter who was 7 and add on childcare for my son. It was not possible.

As a result, I had to agree to allow my son to live with his dad until I could better my circumstances. I took him back when he was 6 and basically overcompensated for having to "give him up" three years prior. I think I'm still doing that to this day."

~ ~

"I will never ever give a child a 16th birthday party. My oldest and her friend ruined that for me. I also learned how to say NO!!! They knew after asking 3 times I would say yes. But, now I learned No!"

~ ~

On a daily basis, I am learning something new about my children. Every day I learn something new about myself. That is what lessons are for; to teach us more about ourselves and the world around us. To become better people, to raise better people, and to help make the communities that we live in better.

Now write your own lessons learned…

_____

_____

_____

_____

_____

_____

_____

_____

_____

_____

_____

_____

_____

_____

_____

_____

_____

_____

_____

_____

_____

_____

_____

_____

_____

_____

_____

_____

_____

_____

_____

_____

_____

_____

_____

_____

_____

_____

_____

_____

_____

« Chapter 8: Mom Support »

"Love Makes a Family"

When I look back on everything that I have been through, I wouldn't be able to accept a "Best Mom" award without listing all those people that helped and supported me through my process. Being a good mother isn't something that just happens when you give birth. It is something that you work at each and every day. I tell people all the time. I wake up every morning and make a decision to be a good mom providing for the needs of my children. I try and fit in some of my needs. (This doesn't always happen every day, but I am a work in progress). You have to choose it; there is not an automatic button that switches into gear.

My mommy squad...

There is something to be said about support when you are a mom. Some moms are forced or choose to be a mommy all by themselves. I would venture to say that those who choose to do it alone have not allowed themselves to be open to help. I can say that I push myself a lot to be the best mom that I can be. I often try to do as much of it all as I can. But as the boys have gotten older, I have accepted the fact that I can't be everywhere at the same time. When the kids were younger, it was easier because Jackson was a baby and couldn't do much but go with the flow while I traveled with Jordan.

Now that they both have their own personalities and interests, it has become more challenging. I try to find things that they both like so they can do them together. But even in those situations, they are at varying degrees of experience or age groups. So we are either forced to come on different days or at different times.

When I was growing up, I despised how involved my parents were with everything. Always asking questions, always around. But now I see that same torture as a God send. Throughout all of my transitions in my personal life, my family has been a constant. Always there to help with anything that I could need from them. They will offer me a break even though I will never ask for one. They have always supported my dreams even when I felt like I couldn't accomplish. Knowing that it would pull me away from my time with the boys. I wanted to open a children's boutique; they offered to compensate where ever I needed them to whether it was picking up from school or taking to a sporting event, or building fixtures. Having support around you also gives you that push to keep moving forward. I am a queen at hiding in plain sight but because I have let people in even just to help with the boys they have become a support and motivational for me as well. They know the goals and are always willing to give encouraging words or tough love when I become distracted.

~ ~

"My main supporter through ALL my challenges, directions, and redirections, has been GOD.

When my kids and I finally moved to a bigger place after my separation and me getting a better job, it was a struggle. I was making more money but my expenses increased more than my income. I ended up getting a part-time job to supplement my income. Unfortunately, I was in a car accident and my car was totaled! If that wasn't bad enough, I find out in the weeks to follow that my "wasband" had cancelled me from our auto policy, and my kids and I from the medical and dental plans. It had only been two weeks since we separated. I had no coverage at all. As a result, I had to pay for rear-ending the car in front of me even though she was at fault.

Well, I considered that being at rock bottom. GOD disagreed. I received a nice check in the mail from a car I had 6 years prior who was financed by a company that had just settled a class action lawsuit. My problem was solved. Ever since that time, I recognize and acknowledge his hand on my shoulder and his support of my life."

~ ~

"At the time he wasn't my husband but a good friend introduced to me by my ex-husband's sister. I wasn't really looking to be in a relationship. I had just gotten out of an awful marriage which took a toll on my mental health and my view on men in general. I told myself that I would never be in a situation to depend on another man. I was going to move forward with my daughter, and I would take care of her. Of course, that was "my" plan, but it wasn't God's plan for her life nor mine. She was going to have an active dad whether I wanted it or not at the time. When he came into our lives, it was quiet and accepting. He was there for whatever we needed. At the time I didn't have a car and walked great distances to get to work, daycare, and the store. He was in the Navy but had a car that he didn't use during the week. He offered to let me use his car while he was on the ship. I just had to agree to pick him us when he was off duty. This man has never stopped supporting me even after marriage and having another child. No matter what I have wanted to do or try or even the struggles, I had finding myself. He has always made it clear that he will do whatever he has to do to make sure that his girls were taken care of. He is our blessings from God."

~ ~

"I've been blessed immensely by having a solid and rational support system. The moms who support me include my own mother, some beloved aunts, and a few close friends. My mother keeps me grounded and is always encouraging. She always seems to say the right thing at the right moment to give me that extra boost of confidence and reassurance that I'm doing alright as a mom. My aunts do the same. Just knowing that other moms I admire, believe that I'm doing a good job, means a lot. I have two friends who share many of the same beliefs I do as a mom. They worked hard to like me, to raise well mannered, intelligent and well-rounded children. It's wonderful to share a collective sigh at the end of the day and words of encouragement amongst each other."

~ ~

Learn to never be afraid to let people help you. Being a successful mom includes having a successful team and support system around you. They are offering to help because they want to. Don't feel like you are inadequate when you ask for some time or someone offers to provide you with some. For those who have an amazing support team already make sure you tell them how much you appreciate them. Love brings people together.

Now write what your support looks like…

_____

_____

_____

_____

_____

_____

_____

_____

_____

_____

_____

_____

_____

_____

_____

_____

_____

_____

_____

_____

_____

_____

_____

_____

_____

_____

_____

_____

_____

_____

_____

_____

_____

_____

_____

_____

_____

_____

_____

_____

_____

_____

« Chapter 9: Mom Balance »

"Mombie –

(n.) A sleep deprived supermom who feeds on caffeine and survives on sticky kisses and messy smiles. Mombies are master multi-taskers and suck it uppers."

-Mombie clothing

Motherhood is a constant act of juggling. I find myself like the plates spinner at the carnival on most days. I have about 10 plates spinning at all times; some faster than others but they are always spinning. As a plate becomes more important it is moved closer to the front while the lesser of important ones hang out in the back. But they are all spinning, and I am always trying to be aware of what is going on with each of them.

My mommy balance…

Being a mom means accepting that no matter what you might have planned or thought you were going to get done can and will change without any notice. I started living on my newly revised block schedule and had planned out what needed to get accomplished tonight during my business block and then enters Jackson. For those who don't know, he is my 5-year-old baby boy. But if he tells it "he's a man" at least a little one anyway.

Jackson: "mommy, my tummy hurts."

Being a mom of 2 and he's the youngest, I have heard this line before as bedtime is approaching and more fun time is being requested.

Me: "Ok, Jackson how about you go lay down for a little bit and see how your feel."

Jackson: "Ok, mommy." (He goes into his room)

15 minutes later….he enter the room

Jackson: "Mommy, my tummy hurts."

I put down the book that I was reading about trademarking.

Me: "Ok, well come lay down, and we can snuggle until you fall asleep."

Jackson: "Ok, as he gets into bed with me." (a slight smile on his face)

After a few minutes, he gets bored with my bed and wants to back to his own room. I go to call my oldest son, Jordan who is 9 came to me. He said, "Mommy, Jackson is in the bathroom throwing up, and it is everywhere."

At that moment I knew that my blocked business work time was over, and I began to prepare for a long night. When your child is sick, a younger child can't always articulate exactly what is going on with him. You learn quickly that you must stay on alert until the sickness has passed. No deep sleep for me.

As I write this at midnight and have cleaned up several disgusting trips to the bathroom, he is now clean, comfortable, in my bed and sleeping. I love him just as much as the moment they put him in my arms.

This is just one example of the many times that my business has to take a backseat to my children. There will always be times where unexpected occurrences will require that you re-adjust previously planned activities to another time and sometimes even another day. At that moment I was a little frustrated. Not at all with my son as he couldn't help that he wasn't feeling well. So, I took a deep breath and reminded myself that the reason I love being a mom in business is that I have the flexibility to spend time with my children and take care of their needs.

~ ~

"As a mother of grown children, I have no idea how I was able to balance all that I had to do versus what was required of me. Without the support of GOD, my family, friends and baby-daddy's, my story would have turned out vastly different. But it didn't, and I'm grateful."

~ ~

"I really missed being a mom having to work swing shifts. So after the birth of my 2nd child. I started working midnight shift. So I could get them off to school, do school trips, pick them up, homework and dinner. I sacrificed so that I could raise my girls. It really helped that my husband only worked 9 days a month. It worked in our favor."

~ ~

"Honestly, I haven't found a way to balance truly being a mom with having a social life. I hardly ever go out alone to socialize with other moms. I'm currently working full time and have three active boys to care for while my husband is deployed. Sadly, social time for myself hasn't been a priority. I need to change that. I'm a rather introverted person, so any free time I have, I enjoy reading or writing, and those are solitary activities."

~ ~

I believe that God gave the ability to do more than one thing at a time. I also believe that with that ability we have to learn to balance that time. Balance is something that I really struggle with. I always felt like there was never enough time in the day to get everything done. What I didn't realize was that it wasn't my lack of time but my lack in prioritizing what needed to be done. As I get better at giving each to do list item its own time I find my stress level decreasing.

Now write your own juggling act story...

_____

_____

_____

_____

_____

_____

_____

_____

_____

_____

_____

_____

_____

_____

_____

_____

_____

_____

_____

_____

_____

_____

_____

_____

_____

_____

_____

_____

_____

_____

_____

_____

_____

_____

_____

_____

_____

_____

_____

_____

_____

_____

« Chapter 10: Hardest Mom Moments »

"From every wound, there is a scar, and every scar tells a story. A story that says. I SURVIVED."

-Craig Scott

A few of us moms know that life can be challenging. At some point in the journey, we are going to be faced with a difficult situation. The good part about knowing this is we also know that it won't last forever. We will be better because of it. At least, this is what we continue to tell ourselves until we see the reasoning or the better on the other side.

A hard mom moment...

A hard time for me as a mother was when I knew that it was over between me and my husband. I have seen so many people struggle with what that looks like for their children. Will he still be around? Will he still take the same care with them like when we were together? Should I stay? I have two sons who need their father in their life. Will I be strong enough to do this by myself? While I was married, I would look into my son's eyes and know that the mother looking at them wasn't giving them everything that they needed because she wasn't whole. The person looking at them was married and wasn't whole. Even when I had a smile on my face, I was sad all the time. I was compromising myself for the love of my children. A fantasy that I had created to say that no matter what he did he was my husband and my children needed their father. Deep down I was afraid that not only would they grow up without their father's constant attention but I would never be happy again. I had two children. Who would love me? The strength of these feeling lasted well after we separated and had decided to file for divorce. Until the day my eldest son looked at me and said, mommy, I am glad you are happy now. At his young age, he had no idea the struggles that we had now that we were on our "own", but he knew that deep inside his mommy wasn't sad anymore. That was enough for me.

~ ~

"Honestly, the hardest moments I feel I've had as a mom are here and now. I have an African American son that I'm justifiably afraid won't come home to me one night. I taught him about courtesy, respect for authority and others and to think before he acts. Even still, if someone else, law enforcement or civilian, is not having the best day or doesn't think before he acts, I could be one of those mother's we see on TV every week, crying and asking why my son."

~ ~

"When my 14 yr old looked at me in total dismay. She began to separate from the family. It really made me question myself. But really she couldn't understand why a man who was supposed to be her father didn't want her. It was hard to see your child try to come to terms with her emotions. It was a challenging time in life for both her and me."

~ ~

"One of the hardest moments I've had as a mom is staying strong for my sons when they're dad deploys. It is not always easy, to exhibit strength and tenacity when it feels like the weight of the world is on your shoulders. It has been particularly challenging now that I'm a full time working mom again."

~ ~

The hardest moments we have as parents are the greatest lessons. Take your time. Go through the process. Then find someone to share your story with. That person will have a hardest moment as well, and they will need your story to remind them that it's ok to have a hardest moment. They will survive just like you did.

Now share your own hardest moment story…

_____

_____

_____

_____

_____

_____

_____

_____

_____

_____

_____

_____

_____

_____

_____

_____

_____

_____

_____

_____

« Chapter 11: Mom Embarrassing Moments »

"I smile because you're my mother. I laugh because there is nothing you can do about it!"

Part of being a mother is being able to laugh at yourself and sometimes laughing at your mistakes. There are moments when your children will do something that makes you want to cry because you are so embarrassed. At the moment you might feel anger or red with shame, but when you look back on it, it's really just a funny story to tell.

An embarrassing moment...

I was at the hospital with my first child. It was mid-January, and it had been snowing. We headed to the hospital as my contractions had picked up. Once at the hospital, they couldn't decide if they were going to send me home which was about 25 minutes away or if they would just keep me as it was snowing. They finally made the decision to let me stay. I was relieved. Labor continued, I received my epidural and found myself some relief. I had my whole family with me in the room. Both my parents and sister were there to support me. The time came closer for my son to make his appearance. They started to prepare the room, and I watched my parents prepare to meet their new grandson. You could feel their excitement. Prior to getting to this point, the nurses had been in several times to check on me. This was my first child I didn't really know what to expect. They were preparing the room for pushing, and I started to feel the pains of my contractions again. I asked the nurse if this was normal.

The nurse informed me that there was a chance that my epidural had worn off, and it was too late to obtain anymore medicine to counteract the pain. My sons head was almost out. They told me to stop pushing because the doctor hadn't arrived yet, I looked at her like she had two heads. Once the doctor arrived it was within a couple pushes and my son was born. Once I finally got my bearings together after the pain, I realized that my dad had filmed the whole thing. Embarrassment set in, and I looked at my dad and said, "you weren't supposed to be down there."

~ ~

"This is gross, but it is without a doubt my most embarrassing moment!! While in labor with my daughter, I had the most incredible urges to push as most moms know. I was holding back as long as I could until it was incontrollable! In the room were my mom, my significant other, the doctor and nurse. I pushed and went to the bathroom from both ends!! My pee went up and over the table, and all I remember is everyone's eyes watching its path to the floor. Then my mom says "Oooh Sherri. That was very nasty!!"

~ ~

"I can recall my 4 year old following behind a disabled woman with a limp and coping the woman.

Understand that I worked midnights so on occasion I would be late picking up my kindergartener who only went for a half day. She would be sitting in the office. I was embarrassed because she told them I was home sleep and when I wake up I was coming. After a couple of times I just learned to stay at the school and helped out for the half day.

Oh, we can't forget about my child who wasn't at an age to be able to count wanted 10 cookies and because she believed she didn't get all ten cookies. She sat on the floor and kicked and screamed, "I want 10 cookies." She had a bag of cookies. I couldn't spank her in the mall, but oh boy wait until we got to the car. Let's just say her father protected her from my embarrassing rage. She got no cookies that day."

~ ~

The embarrassing stories are those that you get to hang over your child's head for the rest of their lives. They are the reason we pull out the cell phone or the photo albums to show family and friends. These are the school pictures that you beg your parents to burn. But they insist on showing your boyfriend. These are the stories that in the moment you just wish it happened to someone else, but over time are a great laugh.

Now write your own embarrassing story...

_____

_____

_____

_____

_____

_____

_____

_____

_____

_____

_____

_____

_____

_____

_____

_____

_____

_____

_____

_____

_____

_____

_____

_____

_____

_____

_____

_____

_____

_____

_____

_____

_____

_____

_____

_____

_____

_____

_____

_____

_____

_____

_____

« Chapter 12: Turning Point »

"Your breaking point is really your making point."

Turning points are those moments in life where you know with everything in you that you can't go backwards. This is the time to change something major about yourself and sometimes your situation. Turning points are huge in how we process significant moments of our lives. No matter the nature or extremity of the cause, the effect is ever changing to everything that we know and sometimes love.

My turning point....

I am 28 years old, married, two children, working full time and running a local children's consignment boutique and in the process of the hardest transition of my life. Making the decision that the fight for my marriage and keeping my family together was over. I watched something that I had worked so hard to keep together fall apart as if it was a movie and I was sitting and watching the drama play out. I watched the inconsistency, the disrespect, and the loss of my peace. I remember sitting down at our dining room table to talk about where our relationship was headed. I remember thinking all I want him to say is he is willing to go to counseling and work on our issues. As we sat there and he began to speak, in my mind I could hear, "I want to keep our family together," but what was actually coming out of his mouth was, "I think we are too far gone for any kind of reconciliation." In that moment, I broke into a million pieces. I found comfort in a dream that I had a few months prior. God said to me no matter what happens I have and will protect you and the boys. Reality told me that this was going to be the hardest thing I have ever experienced, and the transitions and adjustments were going to be stacked on top of each other. But, I knew that the boys and I would get through it and be better for it. This conversation changed my life forever.

~ ~

"During my lowest moment. A time where I had just separated from my husband. Now a single parent, I learned quickly about sacrifice and the choices that I would make for him. Money was getting very tight. One night while cooking dinner, I made a plate for my son. I watched as he engorged the food. He eats a lot and he wanted more. I went back to the pot and realized that there was only enough for one more serving. I put the food on the plate and gave it to my son. The moment changed me, I was never more motivated to never hit this place again. Never again will I have to choose between feeding my child and feeding myself."

~ ~

"I've had several turning points, but the one thing I realized is when a mother is tried and tested to provide for her kids, she will always find a way!

I have no idea in retrospect, how I got from my divorce situation to where I am today, strong, independent and confident about the future. I had moments of near panic attacks because I had two mouths to feed and broke until payday that was 6 days away. But here I sit. In the best financial situation, I've ever been in."

~ ~

"My divorce was tough on me. I felt like it came out of nowhere. We made the decision to get married. We made the decision to add to our family. But after my husband had a stroke everything changed. His love and devotion to the family became monetary and eventually inexistent. After sometime we eventually separated and ultimately divorced. My daughter and I lived in an apartment alone in a city where I had no family and very few friends.

For a long time, I walked in a daze. I continued to take care of our physical needs like working, daycare, grocery shopping but inside I could feel myself slipping away. It came to a point that I thought about taking my life and ending all of the pain. I remember one night sitting on the floor and believing that ending my life would be the only way to make this pain stop. At that moment I thought about my daughter. Who would know that she was here if I did this? Who would take care of her? It would be days for anyone knew she or I were even in this apartment.

The turning point for me was when I surrendered my ex-husband and all my problems to the Lord. I felt free, and my life changed for the better. I began to live again."

~ ~

"Not until I got married did I seriously consider having a family and becoming a mom. My husband and I talked about having a family, and how many children we'd like to have before marrying. But the realization that I was going to be a mom did not set in until after taking the first pregnancy test and seeing a positive result. After being in labor for 23 hours and delivering my son naturally, I realized that I was far stronger than I ever imagined and that motherhood for me, fit like a second skin. Holding my son for the first time, feeling the warmth of his little body on my chest, speaking to him to reassure him that everything was ok and that he was safe in my arms, is a moment that will stay with me forever. That moment changed everything!"

~ ~

Our turning point stories are the stories that miracles are sometimes built on. There were so many stories where a turning point catapulted the mom into a miraculous comeback. A miraculous epiphany where they were able to see clearer what they really wanted their life to look like.

Now write your own turning point story...

_____

_____

_____

_____

_____

_____

_____

_____

_____

_____

_____

_____

_____

_____

_____

_____

_____

_____

_____

_____

_____

_____

_____

_____

_____

_____

_____

_____

_____

_____

_____

_____

_____

_____

_____

_____

_____

_____

_____

_____

_____

« Chapter 13: Disgusting Moment »

"I smile because I'm your child. I laugh because there's nothing you can do about it."

Motherhood constantly tests your endurance and limits. There are moments where you have to encounter some of the most disgusting interactions that your children might bring to you. From picking up random things off the ground to picking their noses and bringing it to you.

A disgusting mommy moment…

When my boys were smaller, I would say about 7 and 3, they decided they wanted to begin to explore their noses. I didn't have any idea that this disgusting new exploration had invaded my house until I went into the boy's room one afternoon. They shared a room, and I decided to mix things up and change their room design. As I began to sit and decide where I wanted to move the furniture, I noticed something going down the wall. At first, I thought one of them must have stuck or spilled something on the wall. As I went over to see what it was, I realized that they were boogies dried on the wall. I was thoroughly disgusted. When I called the boys to the room to find out who and why they had stuck them on the wall. They looked at me and said, "Mommy, they are sticky what else should I have done with them?" Of course, this led to a long conversation about why this was disgusting and where they should go from then on.

~ ~

"My son was a few months old, and I was being to develop my "groove" as a mother. It was a hot summer afternoon, and we were just hanging around the house in out comfy clothes. While enjoying my mommy time with my baby, I realized that he needed to be changed. So as I got up to take him upstairs to change his diaper. I realize that his diaper had already leaked his poop all down my arm and side. At that moment of disgust, I look down at him and realize that he is so calm and happy. Almost as if he was at peace with what he has done. So, of course, I get him all cleaned up followed by myself."

~ ~

"I breastfed my first son, and in the early stages, his poop seemed to be a rainbow of colors. One time, in particular, I'd nursed him while watching a television show. Suddenly, I felt warm and wet across my belly. When I lifted my son up slightly to see if he had peed on me, I realized that not only had he peed, but he had also colored my shirt with hued mustard poop."

~ ~

"The girls were young I would say 10 and 5. We lived in a nice kid-friendly neighborhood, and they were outside playing with their sidewalk chalk and play doh. Thinking nothing of it except they were having fun and were quite I continued cooking and cleaning. After a few hours, it was time to come in for dinner. I walked to open the glass door and realized that they had smashed the play doh into the steps that come into our house. The play doh was so stuck; it took months of scrapping and rain, to get their pretty creation off my steps. They were never allowed to play with play doh again at the house. I remember being in the store with my daughter buying things for my grandchildren and reminded her of this experience with play doh. She immediately put the play-doh back on the shelf."

~ ~

Disgusting mommy moments are your first introduction into mommy hood. They show up when you least expect them and at the most embarrassing time. As a good mom, you try to avoid situations where your motherhood could be seen in a bad light. When your children are born, they are not given the memo that they should keep the disgusting moments for when you are in the privacy of your own home. That would be too easy, and motherhood is never easy.

Now write your own disgusting mommy story...

_____

_____

_____

_____

_____

_____

_____

_____

_____

_____

_____

_____

_____

_____

_____

_____

_____

_____

_____

_____

_____

_____

_____

« Chapter 14: New Addition Mom Moments »

"A new baby is like the beginning of all things – wonder, hope, a dream of possibilities."

-Eda J. LeShan

Getting married is exciting but like most newlyweds know, as soon as you get back from your honeymoon, there are going to be those people that start to ask "when are you having a baby." Then you have those moms who have already had one child, and the baby is walking, and you get the "when are you adding another one." Sometimes it isn't even a conversation. It is more of a surprise and you are expectantly blessed with a new addition. Anyway that the new addition happens is a great moment and memory.

My baby story…

Early on my husband and I talked about if we would have another child. At the time he had a 5-year-old son, and I had a 2-year-old son which we were attempting to successfully blend. Already a pretty complete and busy family of 4, we discussed possibly having one or two more in the future. To our surprise, we came back from our honeymoon, and I was pregnant. We were really excited about the news. Since I had gone through the process and knew the pregnancy routine, I wasn't really worried and felt pretty good. After attending my first doctor's appointment, I felt great and continued on. After a few weeks, I started to spot and we later found out I was having a miscarriage. This was really tough on me. Later that year we decided actually to try to add to our family. It didn't take long and once again we were pregnant.

~ ~

"While discussing our relationship and the desire to get married, the subject of children came up. My husband comes from a family of four children, and I, only two. I knew all along that I didn't want to have a lot of children, so when my husband said he wanted four children, I immediately said no. I told him that two was all I wanted, but that I would compromise, and have three. And if, and only if, the third pregnancy resulted in twins that would be the only way my husband would get his wish of four children. Amazingly, he says he doesn't recall saying he wanted four children. I'll never forget the conversation. Today we have three beautiful boys, and I couldn't be more proud."

~ ~

"New additions to motherhood come in so many different ways. When I first met my future husband I knew that he had a son but didn't really know what that translated into until our first date. I had just started a new job and was very focused on being successful at it as I had a 6-month-old son at home. So when he first asked me out I was very cautious and just really didn't want to out with him. I heard about his reputation when it came to women and that wasn't what I was looking to be attached too. Of course my no made him more persistent, and we became friends and talked for almost two years before we actually went out on a date.

When I finally agreed to go out I wanted it to be public and not so romantic. So we agreed to meet at a Fall Festival with the kids. That was the moment that I not only realized how much I enjoyed his company, but I met his son and loved him too. As I was thinking about dating him it was a constant battle between can I handle two kids? He had his son every other weekend so I believed that it wouldn't be so bad of a transition. In some ways I was right in so many ways, I was wrong. What so many people don't realize is weekend parenting is tough if you are a parent that actually cares about the child being somewhat balanced. In our case we lived in Baltimore, he lived with his mom in Laurel. That is about a 45 minute separation. He was very active in sports. I wanted him to feel at home with us and to do that I felt like I needed to make sure that we attended as many of his activities as we could. So when the season schedules were released for sports, I would pray that the boy's schedules didn't overlap.**"**

~ ~

Not every new additions story is traditional and starts with a birth plan. Some happen just because you love another person and want to spend the rest of your life with them. The conversations that are had are similar but oh so different. You are dealing with a life that already exists, that already has a mother or father to make decisions. You might feel like the outsider but always remember as long as you love the child and have their best interest the rest will fall into place.

Now write your own new additions story…

_____

_____

_____

_____

_____

_____

_____

_____

_____

_____

_____

_____

_____

_____

_____

_____

_____

_____

_____

_____

_____

_____

_____

_____

_____

_____

_____

_____

_____

_____

_____

_____

_____

_____

_____

_____

_____

_____

_____

_____

_____

_____

« Reflections »

"Behind every great kid is a Mom who's pretty sure she's screwing it all up."

       I have always had a passion for families. No matter the dynamic of the family; a passion for each family to find a way to cater holistically to the needs of everyone in the family. I really believe that the small moments really matter just as much as the bigger moments.

       This book was birthed out of the idea that so many times as moms we don't share or have the opportunity to share some of the real and raw moments that we have raising our children. Every mom's experience with motherhood is different as we all make different choices and have different priorities as we travel the maze. But we can learn from each other. We can take these stories and relate them to our own lives. If it is an experience that we haven't had and might not have, I hope that there is a lesson learned that each of you could take away from it.

       What is also important is that I ask that if you see a topic that we didn't discuss that you would join our Facebook group or email us your stories. All stories are anonymous and free from any judgment. The goal is not only to help rear children into whole and thriving adults but for their parents to experience that same kind of freedom.

Join us in the H.E.Y. Mom Community

- Did you like what you read?

- Do you have some stories to share with other moms?

- Do you feel like you would like to read more?

- Do you want to connect with other moms?

Contact Us:

www.heyyouthinc.com

info@heyyouthinc.com

Follow Us:

@ mommymazerunner

@ heyyouthinc